Transforming the Moment

Margrit Dahm

A Meditation on God's Love and the Fullness of Life

First Published 2016 by:
Matthew James Publishing Ltd
19 Wellington Close
Chelmsford
Essex
CM1 2EE
www.matthewjamespublishing.com

ISBN: 978 1 910265-25-3

Printed in the UK by 4edge

'Poetry slices into life, clearing away the layers of what has become second-hand, derivative and an escape from meaning rather than an encounter with it as an alive presence. Margrit Dahm also tunes her simple and transparent poems to what she discovers over and over in her daily practice. This is why she communicates something timeless, but in a voice that is fresh and surprising.'

Laurence Freeman

Laurence Freeman OSB
Meditatio House
32 Hamilton Road
London W5 2EH, UK
www.wccm.org

Preface

John Main OSB (1926-1982) who rediscovered meditation in the Christian tradition for us states in his book 'Community of Love': "There is only one way we can judge our progress, and that is by the quality of our love."

Indeed the fruits of meditation are the same as the fruits of the spirit mentioned in the Holy Scripture: love, peace, joy, patience, kindness, compassion and self-control

I have followed this path of meditation for a good many years now, and it seems to me a natural progression that I was able to write the poems presented here in as much as they were influenced by and have grown out of my daily practice.

The poems are predominantly short and therefore can invite the reader to spend some time reflecting on them and contemplating their meaning.

Margrit Dahm

Contents

Every moment

Every moment
which is given us
is an opportunity to be
awake and receptive.

When we wake up from
the hypnotic sleep
which keeps
the world imprisoned,

we will welcome
God's loving gift,
and it will transform us
into the liberty
of the children of God.

My offering

Oh source of my life,

may my aim always be
to serve and rest in thee;

guard my mind from too much noise
that wants to undermine your voice;

in your presence let me speak
that which with my soul I always seek,

and when one day from here I part,
let your love enfold my heart.

Be ready!

Sit down swiftly on his behest
and gently close your eyes,
then behold what can never be expressed,
but which once you knew and knew its prize;

let your inner self be filled
and let it thoroughly refresh you,
and your thirst which will thus be stilled
will favour what you will pursue;

for when you then resume your day's activity
your inner strength will further it,
you will feel freed of enmity
and a steady flame will in your heart be lit.

Constancy

May I always feel free to go
in and out of my Father's house,

may his presence follow me
whenever I will leave,

and when I then return once more
I ask that it may bring

the kind of joyful peace to me
which only he knows how to give.

Understanding

When a gulf opens up
between you and someone close,
descend into its darkness

and when you rise again,
you may understand better
what's keeping you apart.

Self-will

Whenever your actions and words
are not pleasing in the eyes of God,

they were not driven by love,
but far more likely

they arose
out of your own self-will.

Being comforted

If anything wants to disturb your heart
and has unsettled you,

bring it before the Lord
and he will comfort you,

for whatever comes to rest in his hands,
is sure to have lost its sting.

Your enemies

When you begin to meet
the enemies inside of you

don't dismiss them
nor reject them,

but come to love them
for they, too, can learn
to serve the Lord.

Passive and active

When we are confronted
with hostile and hurtful remarks,

we want to react and respond
immediately in the same
passive way – we bear grudges,
get angry, foster resentment…

But when we make instead
an effort of consciously
embracing the offence
in an act of love,

we will be able
to forgive what was
and focus on that which is.

Like

Whenever my prayer is incomplete,
pray, take it in your hands
and let it rest there
in all its imperfection,

and like the weightless feather of a bird
which when touched upon
by the sun's enlivening rays,
displays the spark
of iridescent colours,

so the silence of my prayer
will quietly unfurl beneath the wing
of your perfection
and find its meaning
in your unfailing love.

About change

We cannot change the world
but we can change ourselves.

In order to change ourselves
we have to wake up,

and in order to wake up
we must know that
we often fall asleep.

Always

The goodness of God
and the goodness of his creation
can never be destroyed,

it will always stand erect
as Jesus stood erect
in the midst of his accusers.

A light

In the obscurity of the night
a light awaits you
which shines brighter
than the day.

Your inner eye

When you look
at your surroundings
with the patience
of your inner eye

the world immediately
becomes
a better place.

About care

Teach me
to care
and not to care:
teach me
to be still.

About love

Love is the great peacemaker
transformer and healer -
it teaches us equanimity,
understanding and kindness,

and in order to be open
to its infinite wisdom
we must want to give up
what stands in its way.

About negativity

You may be hurt, bruised
rejected, criticised or angry –

yet if you don't give in,
but stay with these emotions
and become aware of them,

their negativity will be disarmed,
and their energy is
redirected and transformed.

Evening praise

When the day draws to a close
I join the birds to sing your praise

and as all unsettled haste
begins to find its resting place

your living breath
comes down on me.

Spoken words

Harsh words,
words which want to hurt,
to disconcert,
to negate and destroy what is

can be deprived of their power
if you can stay focused
and let them pass,
holding fast to your love,
trusting in God's endless mercy,

and they will be discharged and
sent back to the futile existence
from which they had emerged.

Trust in Him

If the door has been shut,
the Lord will use the keyhole
to let his love flood in.

About truth

A net of untruth
cannot last:

a minor gust of wind from above,
and the net is torn to shreds;

now the light of truth
can no longer be denied.

To forgive

When the spirit of forgiveness
has entered our heart,
we are also able to say:
'I am sorry' –

first for our own faults,
and then for the faults of the other.

Now

When mind and heart
are joined together,

stillness and silence
open up before me,

and I can breathe in
the present moment.

Those moments

Those moments spent
in the here and now

are, despite
their interruptions,

first gathered and then
worked into a string of pearls.

All desires

When we are in the presence
of the Lord, all our desires,
as though captured by
a great central force, are
fused together in the one wish:
to stay and rest in Him.

And yet

How small is our understanding,
how negligent our insight
into matters of divine love,

and yet, when the Holy Spirit
takes hold of us,
we know everything
we are given to know
in an instant.

Guide me

Guide me, please, to your kingdom,
and when I cross the threshold,
let me do so
with humility and infinite joy.

The beauty

When we come to experience
the presence of the Divine
in our own hearts,

we also realise
that the beauty
of all works of art

is already deeply embedded
in God's creativity and love.

Invocation

As I do in the stillness
of my meditation,

the chorus of the birds
invokes their Creator
in his creation
in the early evening hours

and lets the gentle voice
of love and euphonic
harmony be known.

Simile

We could compare it
with the way a house is built
when we seek a life lived in fullness:

we must first have a good foundation –
we need a good discipline,

and with each meditation
we then begin to build the house
brick by brick;

when we put on the roof, it will
shield us from any great adversity,

and we are finally ready
to inhabit the house we have built.

I must

I must melt into the background
so that the presence of Christ
can come to the fore in me –

and his love will then lead me
to the Father – in Him everything
that has been created
is forever unified.

In stillness and silence

My heart will not cease
to sing the praises of the Lord,

and in response, his indwelling
spirit answers with her love

thus creating a sense of
unity and joy.

Movement and stillness

There is a constant murmuring out there,
like fountains bubbling, effervescing,
and hearing becomes listening

when the wind sweeps through the foliage –
can it accentuate or assuage
the passage of time,
whenever in a wave of motion
it breaks away
from the still point's expansive ocean?

Each gust of wind is likely
to betray its inherent fullness
by giving itself completely,
and being thus consumed, it readily
returns to the realm of
unmoving calm and stillness

until a modulated force will once more revive
and stir it to a renewed surge of life.

A landscape

Our heart is
a landscape
that loses itself in the eternal,

and the light from above
gives it colour, lucidity and definition.

Linked

Life and death –
alpha and omega
join hands together
and lead us to immortality.

In the heart

When we leave behind
the complexity of our mind

and enter the simplicity
and silence of the heart,

the expanse of divine love
which has awaited our arrival

comes to meet us within the
narrow confines of our humanity.

Our path

Treading our path
with the simplicity of a child
and the clarity of an easy mind

will lead us deeper and deeper
into the immensity and mystery
of God's unbounded love.

Your joy

Joy sinks into my heart
when I hear your voice:

in the music I am listening to,
the bird singing its evening praise,

and in the words of those
who are close to me.

Our life's work

Our life's work should be
not unlike a tree:

always seeking the light,
always rising upward,

it lifts its branches up
to the sun.

Not yet

As long as we cannot see
that our faults are as manifold
and varied as those
of our neighbour,

who I am about to criticise,
we have not yet understood
the full meaning of humility.

Only

Slander is indeed very hard to endure,
and we find the only effective cure

in those good forces which live within –
they will help to combat this dreadful sin.

Everything

Everything I think or do –
be it important or insignificant –

receives its own particular value
through His presence which

I turn to whenever I sit down
to meditate.

About lying

A lie in its various aspects
is the wall of separation

which prevents us experiencing
the presence of God –

if we are able to turn
and change direction

God will immediately come
to meet us.

Your breath

You are in everything and in all –
and all and everything is with your
living breath imbued;

any path that ever man pursued
wants always to make sure
that he attunes to his Father's call.

When we meditate

The vista which opens up
before us when we meditate
knows no bounds and

reaches far beyond
any vantage point
that we may encounter.

As

As the waters rest
in the infinite depths of the earth,

so we may find in your all-embracing being
the peace and solace which sustain us,

and as the wind
brushes past the ripening heads of corn,

so may your holy spirit touch
the disquieted walls of unending thoughts.

Mindfulness

Mindfulness is
that quality of the heart

where we are able
to become more perceptive

towards ourselves
and the world which
surrounds us.

Creative silence

Nothing seems to change
in our life when we begin to meditate;

and yet, once we enter
into the creative silence

which wants to fill our whole being,
everything is changed.

If. . .

If we keep our eyes
firmly fixed on the divine

and only then turn to
the concerns of the world,

the Lord will be with us
in everything we do,
and we will find peace.

Any situation

Any situation which is
approached with a clenched fist,
will not be resolved peacefully;

if we could but remember
to be present at such moments,
we would be able

to dissolve the tension
and to be calm in the storm.

An undiscovered country

Travelling and returning
to your own heart
unveils an undiscovered country

which is more mysterious
and more radiant than
any holiday resort could ever be.

Please

May I have the gift
to recognise you in your creation
so that I can always make the shift

from the narrow limitation
of motion to the stillness
of your ever-present endlessness.

The peace we wish for

People say: if only
I could live in quiet surroundings,
I would find inner calm and harmony,

and they forget that
the path must lead to your own heart,
where true peace can be found;

then even the thorny part of the way
will not be an obstacle,

and the pain deep inside
will be accepted
because it is resting in good hands.

Rejection

Any rejection we experience
will be balanced out
by the attitude and kindness
of those who are well
disposed towards us,

and God's love which is
always willing to accept us
the way we are
is also telling us:
you are not alone.

Families

Families can be the source
of many joys,
but also of much sorrow

when there are too many
divisive opinions
and too much corrosive
self-interest.

Just as

Different religions
present us with different
facets of the same truth:

just as in a prism
the shaft of light
brings forth a multitude of colours,

so the source of truth is poured
into many tonalities of meaning
only to be gathered in by silence.

Be still

Be still! The Lord is near,
his peace moves before him;

be awake, but do not fear,
for what was once his life's short interim

is still reality for us today –
so be ready, be on your way!

Emptying

The vessel has to be empty
before it can be filled.

Colours and sounds

Summer's glow
is softly blending with
the stillness' gentle breath

and carries in its subtle breeze
the traces of the rainbow's
secret colours –

a bell resounds
in a hazy, far-off distance,

and spreading its wings,
the serenity of the moment

is quietly touching
the life of all that exists.

God's love

To meet and experience
God's love in your own heart
is nothing short of a miracle.

Only

Only selfless love,
love which knows not to be
subjective or resentful,

but simply to be, can truly
forgive the word which was
spoken in defiance and anger;

we don't obtain such love,
it is given to us
as it is already present

in our hearts; but we must
learn to turn towards it by
allowing it to express itself.

Acts of kindness

Much in our life cannot be changed;
but we can pave our way
with lots of little acts of kindness

which will go ahead of us
and by which we will be remembered.

Be aware

When accusation, division
and unseemly words
want to assail you
and engulf the foundation
of your inner peace,

know that
because of the strength
of the force
which is at work within,

the actual hub
of the ailment will soon
die its natural death.

Reflection

Nature always indicates
and points us to
the time which is passing,

but its cycle of the
four seasons
encloses also the circular motion
of Alpha and Omega.

Ready

Up to us the readiness
to receive –
the rest is given.

Whatever happens

The thought
that God is with us
will comfort us in
whatever happens,
be it good or bad.

In his silence

I bring before God
what concerns me at this moment,

and having placed it into his hands
I can rest in his silence.

Advent

His coming can no longer
be delayed now:

so let us prepare a place
for him in our hearts.

Beyond

Beyond likes and dislikes,
beyond affirmation and negation

lies the eternal spring
of unadulterated renewal
and redeeming love.

It is

I think we can best understand
what it is that is forevermore and
in eternity,

when we consider the infinite
capacity of divine love –
it has no beginning and no end,

but is wholly embedded in His
and our being – it simply is.

As though

As though nestling
under the wing of an angel,

I am gently carried into
the presence of the Lord,

and am allowed to remember
that we are children of God.

In you

In you is joy overflowing,
in you is the root of all life,
and your will is always sowing
in us the perfect wish to strive.

You are constantly moving,
nothing in you ever stands still:
worlds are cascading, approving
of days passing by, as is your will.

You are eternal rest,
you are forever stillness and silence,
we step forward at your behest
while angels bow in deference.

Lord, have mercy

Lord, have mercy
on this world and its existence;
see, how it wrestles
and struggles at great pains,
then it calls on you,
and then from you refrains –
oh, give us back our innocence -

it understands and it can tell
what is forever inherently true;
for whatever men may build or may construe,
is but a world in its outer shell,

when at its centre must be you alone;
only then man who is your servant,
will be ready for the endorsement
that he never acts merely on his own,

and unified in you as one community,
we will create a world as you had planned it,
and what man before had just suspected,
will become a strongly felt reality;

together we will set the wheels in motion
and so renew what had lain fallow,
and blessèd will be every furrow,
dissolved the pull of all illusion

About the author

Margrit Dahm lived in Germany before she came to London where she first trained as a teacher and then studied German literature at the University of London. She worked at a language school as a teacher of the German language while continuing her studies in order to obtain a MA degree. She has two children from a previous marriage.

Her publications include two books of German poetry published by Karin Fischer Verlag, Aachen, Germany.

Her autobiography is in the process of being published by Austin Macauley, Canary Wharf, London.